RAIN TO ROOT

RAIN TO ROOT

Poems of meeting grief and grace

KIM BIRDSONG

Foreword by Francis Weller

Sage & Stone Publishing
Carmel, California

Published by Sage & Stone Publishing
Carmel, California

www.kimbirdsong.com

ISBN: 9798218505431

Cover art by Kim Birdsong

Author Photograph by Karl Grobl

Book design and production
by David Gordon
Lucky Valley Press
www.luckyvalleypress.com

Printed in the USA on acid-free paper

for Stephanie,

homing beacon of my heart

~~%o CONTENTS o%~~

CONTENTS *(continued)*

III. ROOTING & RISING

CONTENTS *(continued)*

Imagine! I've had rainbows in my clouds.

— Maya Angelou

FOREWORD

L ove and loss have been eternally entwined, inseparable from one another. There is no love that does not know the gravity of loss and no loss that does not carry the reminders of love. Everything we love we will lose. This is a fierce and unrelenting truth that can cause us to harden the heart against the inevitable pain of loss.

In *Rain to Root,* Kim Birdsong has gifted us with a collection of poems that announce themselves with an authentic voice of someone who has undertaken the deep descent into soul through her encounters with loss. She has kept faith with a prolonged vigil in the darkness. This is not easy work. Kim did not turn away. She made a commitment to let grief reshape her and draw out of her, the depths of soul. She was devoted to working with her sorrow, giving it shape in the forms of these exquisite offerings.

These poems are an act of revelation, a soul offering, and they are simultaneously universal. Kim reveals in these pages her season of acute sorrow following the death of her son. We are reminded by her passages that no one is exempt. Every one of us will have an intimate encounter with loss and death. Every one of us will be brought into the depths through our times of sorrow, feeling the pull downward into the shadowlands of grief. Kim offers us a sense of direction, rooted in her devotional work with grief, gifting us with cairns in the wilderness to help us navigate our own walk into the unknown.

The poems in *Rain to Root* are fierce and tender, heartbreaking and healing. They are love letters that carry the scent of sage and burnt leaves, and sting the throat like powdered glass. They could only be written by someone who has taken a vow to engage fully the depth of our encounters with the dark angel of loss. They could only be crafted by someone who has been initiated by time in the underworld.

Rough Initiation

The death of a child carries a sorrow that is unbearable. I have sat with many parents over the years in my psychotherapy practice and in grief rituals, who have been gutted by this primal loss. When Kim's son died, she was thrown into a *rough initiation;* a period of radical change brought about by the circumstances of her life. Initiations are meant to reshape our identity, breaking us open to a wider and more porous experience of who we are. A rough initiation, however, can shatter us down to the smallest circumference. Similar to traditional initiations, we are broken apart, shaken, and deranged by the experience. However, unlike those rites of passage held within the supportive arms of community and elders, a rough initiation has little to no containment. We feel adrift and lost during these traumatic times, unsure of where to place the next step. "I don't know who I am anymore," is a frequent lament that people share when in the midst of a rough initiation. The familiar stars are no longer available to guide our movements.

Without an adequate container, we can get stuck in a liminal state, leaving us hovering between worlds. Our task is to complete the suspended initiation and experience a return to the community. This is at the heart of these poems. Through art and the poetic imagination, Kim offers us a way to work with our own experiences of a rough initiation. Her faithful wanderings in the dark hallways of soul, led her eventually to new ground. She boldly states, "Let this sorrow be my undoing." Her fidelity to the process of being undone, walking the *via negativa,* where we are remade not by addition, but rather through the work of letting go and subtraction, is a weighty invitation to surrender to the work of soul. Making beauty out of loss is pure alchemy.

Initiation is not optional. Each of us will be taken to the edge of our own ripening through the workings of soul. In the absence of formal communal practices to escort us to the edge of change, psyche will use whatever is present in our lives to lead us to the same ground. The death of a child will certainly take one to the precipice of radical change, provided, however we work with the material that is there. To do this we need to take up *an apprenticeship with sorrow.*

An Apprenticeship with Sorrow

Grief and loss touch us all, circulating around us in a multitude of ways, some deeply personal, some collective in nature. When we acknowledge this truth, we recognize the importance of taking up an apprenticeship with sorrow. We do this so that we can stay present to our lives, remain open to the lustrous beauty of the world, and not be reduced to trying to outrun sorrow.

It takes tremendous psychic strength to engage the wild images, searing emotions, chaotic dreams, grief-stained memories, and visceral sensations that arise in times of deep grief. We must build soul muscle to meet these times with anything resembling affection. *The apprenticeship is long.*

To do this work, we must become skillful in the *art of vesseling.* This comes from an old Alchemical idea that real change requires a reliable holding space within which the heat of transformation can take place. The materials we see in the vessel are the elements connected with our grief: Fear, sadness, anger, hopelessness, love, despair, longing, and others. Our work is to keep the material warm, to offer it our attention, affection, care, compassion, witnessing, and devotion. We must slowly cook the substances until they are ready to change. We can feel these qualities in this collection of poems. They are riddled with affection. Kim has kept the material warm.

After years of walking alongside grief, working with its difficult cargo, we gradually come to see how we have been reshaped by this companionship. We see how we have cultivated a greater interior space to hold more of what life brings to us. What slowly emerges from this long apprenticeship, this vigil with sorrow, is a spaciousness capable of holding it all—the beauty and the loss, the despair and the yearning, the fear, and the love. We become immense: *The apprenticeship patiently crafting an elder.*

Kim writes, "I no longer fear the cost of change." Imagine that. Imagine living with a recognition that life will change us, and what is asked of us in exchange is to collaborate with these alterations in our inner landscape. This is an elder's hard-earned wisdom, tempered by the heat of loss and the willingness to welcome all of what is there.

The vigil is long, the work of sorrow slowly reshaping our inner contours, making us more spacious and capable of holding the wide arc of sorrows that greet us every day. Kim's poems are soul epiphanies, revealing the deeper calling of how to live in this bittersweet world.

This is a prayer book, a meditation, a gathering of potent medicine for the growing Clan of the Brokenhearted. Read them like you would from holy scripture. You have entered sacred ground. Some of these poems will make you tremble in their raw truth telling. Others will call up tears from the cave of the heart "spilling onto Earth, the only altar left."

— Francis Weller
Russian River Watershed
Shasta Bioregion
Author, *The Wild Edge of Sorrow: Rituals of Renewal and the Sacred Work of Grief*

PART I: DOWNPOUR

Windows
miles from the sun
glow gold with its setting.

Precious one,
notice how moonlight dances
on the lake of your tears.

WADE IN

to the waters of grief,
to the currents of regret.
Study the tides of overwhelm.
However daunting it seems to face
what resides in murky depths, risk
a deep dive. Risk descent uncovered, unadorned,
unguarded, undefended. Expose the tender
underbelly, the rawness of pain. Let yourself be
unpeeled, unhinged, unmade, unsure. Your brightest light,
the one beating in your chest, will guide you.
Below, next to the barely bearable and the shunned,
is the man who sells lemon basil at the farmer's market.
The woman buying fish and the temple sweeper,
the nurse and the neighbor are there. You will never be
alone. Notice your ragged breath, the old cries caught
in your throat yearning to fly. Keep dropping.
You may tumble, swirl in a tangled kelp bed
without direction for a time,
but you will not be harmed.
Deeper beneath the surface
is softness, stillness resting inside you, amid
rising tides of rage and confusion.
You will resurface.
You will find your toes in the mud of this shore again.
You will be changed.
Let yourself be
surprised by the unexpected,
by the buoyancy of the heart.

Here, take my hand,
I will go with you.

TIMELESS

There was no time
for a diagnosis to sink in,
for a long term treatment plan,
no time to adjust to diminished
physical ability or new mental state.
There were only 90 minutes
until you were gone,
and then
all there was
was time.

WHEN HE DIED

I couldn't be with him
I couldn't get to him in time
I wasn't there
when he died
There wasn't enough time
I couldn't hold his hand,
    stroke his hair
    or kiss his forehead
    as he died
I couldn't be there
    to hear his breathing slow
    to hear the monitor beep
    its slow confirmation of his
    final moments
I had to decide on the phone
    about pain medication, the breathing tube,
    the option to defibrillate
I wasn't there
    to see his chest rising and falling
    and then not rise again
I couldn't sit with his body
    release his hand
    one last time
    or walk away clutching
    his belongings
    to my chest

I couldn't be there when he died

I didn't want to watch him die
    on a zoom call
        or hold my phone facing the screen
    so my daughter could watch
    or watch my grandson watch his father die
    but I did
    it was the only way
because I couldn't make it in time

I wanted to watch
    despite the collapsed catastrophe
    of his life, our lost connection
I didn't want to watch it end
    but I did
and as I sat watching him
    I saw his spirit,
    the joyful, innocent spark from infancy,
    before everything rushed toward ruin,
    the essence underneath the smile
        he gave me when I snapped
    that utterly perfect picture of him
    wearing the tuxedo onesie
    his godparents sent him
    for his first New Year's Eve.
    I saw it again, that inspirited essence,
    pass across his face
    softening what the world had hardened
    for a fraction of a second
    before it rose and fled.

I have held on to that vision
　　kept it close
　　because I wasn't there
　　when he died
and because it holds the key
to unlocking the gates of compassion and acceptance
I must pass through
to continue living.

THE ONLY ALTAR LEFT

Eons of darkness descended
filling each instant of the moments after he died;
lightyears without light,
ragged truth, an invisible, penetrating bullet
creating shrapnel, rearranging my bones.
I can't tell you how long it lasted.

The shock, the shock, such shock!
A new reality was saturating the world
with unstructured, ungoverned faithlessness.
Here, Yahweh never came to Moses
nor Gabriel to Muhammed.
The boulder never rolled from the crypt.
The Ganges and the Nile, both dry.

Siddhartha remained prince in his kingdom,
never reaching the Bodhi tree.
Persephone never ate the pomegranate seed.
Spring was postponed, interminably delayed,
possibly cancelled altogether.
Olympus merely rock.
Voices, human or animal, couldn't reach ears,
messages from plants, rerouted.

The echo chamber of my heart fell silent,
broken. There's no Novocaine for death,
but under the faithless caul, numbness
was complete.

Sound returned in a wail I didn't know
lived inside, coming from a place I still can't name,

dropping me
to my knees
as the first tears began to fall
spilling onto Earth,
the only altar left.

IN THE LONG DARK

on the days when the reasons
to leave the couch are few
broken
pieces of my heart
cast long shadows
across the floor
Color seems to have bled
from the sky
and holes carved deep in my bones
whistle when the wind blows
and the door I thought
I'd latched securely flies open
and memories
swarm in
some fire, some honey
and the cries only the dog hears
are drowned by the downpour overhead
and tears, hot and heavy,
join the rain
flowing
into the trough
along the side of the street
making their way to the sea,
each drop
part poem
part prayer
part praise
and part pain.

STOP THE WORLD

I remember Mom joking,
when something bad would happen,
eyes and arms to the heavens proclaiming
Stop the world! I want to get off!
I always wondered how that worked.
Oh! What power I would have!
I remember smiling
for the first time
after she died, recalling
her impossible joke.

Forty years later,
like an old ghost swirling past the bedside,
I thought of it again
when my son passed,
thinking this time, *gosh,*
he actually figured it out.
but I don't think,
deep down,
he really meant
forever.

IS THE CELLO WEEPING, OR AM I?

Listening
the tightly pulled knots of
my heartstrings loosen
stretching
unable to hold the beat steady
pulled so far out they snap.
Heartpieces break off
icy shards
too sharp to touch hit
the floor cutting
any piece of me
compelled to retrieve them.

Stunned prisoners suddenly freed
those parts left open
raw   exposed   quivering
reach
the way my son would raise his arms
up to be lifted and held
desperately seeking
my full welcome.

Together, brokenness and I
lean toward a bending light
on the horizon
inviting us to dance
with sorrow and
the redemption it carries.

Reunited, smiles budding
we sway attuning
to a new and ancient rhythm
wetting our feet
in the puddles
left by the ice
melting in the warming
morning light.

SCATTERING

Descent, Sacrifice & Return

I head out at the sound of the morning monastery bells.
You, first born, are in a sack I carry on my back.
There is no other way I can bear your weight.

At the top of the stairs to the beach
two cypress trees grow together:
one, large and sprawling
partly splayed on the ground,
the other standing sturdy,
branches touching overhead,
roots entwined,
gnarled, worn with footfalls,
threshold
to the sand and surf below.

I pause, I pray
then descend,
each step prayer
alert to nature, to her gestures

O my son!

There are witnesses to this journey:

a single gull
perched atop the pointed hat
of the gnome-shaped rock,
a few otters bobbing,
a young pelican
balanced, floating.

You liked blue,
I like green
so I leave you here
where they meet
in the water
under a blue sky
against the deepest green
where an old kelp-covered
goddess boulder opens
and the waves foam
their whitest white,
my body delivering you
to a new world for the last time.

The first pass of the next wave cradled
and held you, kept you close
in a way I never could —
a blessing, a welcome
a salty baptism,
turning the ash of you
the color of palest peach,
bone soup, this mother's offering.
You float while I stare,
worried I had not placed you

far enough away from shore.
Just then
the Pacific surged
fierce, greedy, unexpected,
wave after wave crashing,
making a complete sweep,
taking you and my breath away
absorbing you in
to that impossible whiteness,
churning in the wild-dark depths.

There was no question that you were wanted.

I notice the gull still perched on its rock,
The otters still bobbing in the kelp.
The pelican remained floating. Everything the same,
yet everything utterly changed.

Sack emptied
I pray, I bow,
I walk home,
unable to discern
which one of us has died
and which has been reborn.

I DIDN'T KNOW

that the surf was so high
that it would cover the rocks
where I had scattered your ashes.
I didn't know that the foam would reach
so far up on the sand
or that the clouds would spread themselves
across the sky, strewn cotton loosened
from its bag, in the shape of a wing. I didn't know
the ice plant had begun to flower and that
the first poppies of spring had arrived nestling
between them. I didn't know, couldn't know
until I walked outside, until I sat and breathed
with it, like I didn't know, couldn't have known how wide
my heart would stretch,
needed to stretch,
until you died.

9 MONTHS

Since you passed,
long enough to birth
something,
long enough to understand
that you live in the ocean swell,
that the pieces of you
offered up
have become inseparable
from air
from sand
the dog tracks in,
not quite long enough
to stop asking
the world
why.

YOU LIVE IN ME

after "I Wear You" by Susan Vespoli

You live in my throat like a wail.
You drove a stake through my heart.
You live in my belly like a stone.
You buzz like a bee in my brain.

You drove a stake through my heart,
Your death, the death of all hope.
You buzz like a bee in my brain
in a space between horror and grace.

Your death, the death of all hope,
Your heartbeat stopped on the street
in a space between horror and grace,
spiny cactus I struggle to hold.

Your heartbeat stopped on the street.
There was nothing anyone could do.
Spiny cactus I struggle to hold,
There would be no 37th year.

There was nothing anyone could do.
The clouds hung low in the sky.
There would be no 37th year.
You chased the wrong spirit home.

The clouds hung low in the sky.
We had to say goodbye.
You chased the wrong spirit home.
Your life a candle on my shrine.

We had to say goodbye,
You live in my belly like a stone,
Your life a candle on my shrine,
You live in my throat like a wail.

TUESDAY

after "Sunday" by January Gill O'Niell

Tuesday, really? Tuesday.
Here you are
showing up like a bad penny,
a silent prod to continue.

You are far from ruby, Tuesday.
For God's sake,
your biggest claim to fame is tacos.
I'm rather peeved
by your brazen arrival,
your pathetic attempt at normalcy.
Clearly you've conspired with the sun
to make this wretched day.

How dare you
arrive on the heels of my storm
pretending nothing's wrong
knowing full well
that what came before you
made the bottom drop
and the sky fall.

You are not important.
You are not the day my son died.
You are the day after.
What challenges, beyond breathing,
do you throw down today?

Tuesday, Bloody Tuesday,
don't you know
I wasn't finished being mad at him,
yet life leaked out all the same.

Truly Tuesday, you are something
to endure, like grief.
You bring too much truth
to bear across an endless line of days.
You are something
I'd rather pass through
unscathed,
unnoticed and unremarkable,
like you,
a regular Tuesday
on the way to hump days and fun days.

Maybe I'd rather be commonplace.
Maybe I don't want to be the mother
whose son is dead.
Maybe I shouldn't care if others see me
the way I want to be seen.

Oh, Tuesday,
Maybe none of it matters.
Maybe we're both flummoxed
by the arbitrariness of it all,
by our placement on this planet,
by our inability to turn our backs
on our own existence.

Perhaps, Tuesday, our creator made us
out of curiosity
just to see what we'd do
in the middle of crazy,
and perhaps neither one of us
knows what to do
when the sky falls
and the bottom drops away
when death comes on a Monday

and now it's Tuesday
and I'm out of Kleenex
and running low
on chocolate.

UNDOING

If I don't tend
to the chores
demanding attention,
then the disarray of
my unkempt house
will more accurately match
my inner landscape—
askew
disheveled—
as jumbled as this grief.

Here it should not look
clean nor appear
orderly.
There should be dust,
a thin layer
at the very least,
and a sink full
of unwashed
dishes, piles of
unfolded clothes, unshelved books.
The garbage and the compost pail
need emptying
I need to make dinner,
make the bed.

It is all waiting for me,
but he is not.

Dig out the freshly
poured tar
from the potholes.
Pry it free
from the cracks in the road.
Stop trying to smooth over the world!
Let the ride be bumpy,
unsettling.
Let this sorrow be my undoing.
Allow it all, the road, the house
the clothes, the books, the cries
to be as messy, unorganized,
as disobedient
as this untidy life.

Nothing
really stays
in its place
for long anyway.

Fuck beauty!
Damn a smooth ride.
I have a first class ticket
to the underworld.

Care to join me?

GUESTHOUSE RULES

Rules posted at the entrance
to Rumi's guesthouse
instruct us
to welcome all who appear
to invite them in, arms outstretched

But oh!
I fear there is no more room,
not at this house.
Already guests
sleep 3 and 4 to a bed.
They occupy every chair,
and there are many I must
step over lying
scattered on the floor.
More are resting
on the front lawn.
Still others
have formed a line at the door,

knocking
begging admission
to wreak god knows what havoc
on my heart.
I cannot bear to be swept clean
again.

I do not crave any more adventures
nor desire
yet
another
guide
from beyond!

Do not be fooled by neighbors
bearing their fragrant offerings,
those freshly baked muffins,
the hand cut garden roses,
nor be tempted by the deceitful allure
of the beautiful.
Quickly now!
Lower the shades.
Bolt the door.
Turn off the lights.
Post a bold sign in all caps with red letters:
NO VACANCY.

JESUS LOVES YOU

Hungry, will work for food
Need money for the bus, to feed my children
Experiencing houselessness
Please help
Anything helps
God bless

At the light on the corner
before I turn toward home
a homeless man
is twirling his sign
the way sign walkers do
outside car dealerships and pizza parlors
when they're having a sale.
He's swinging a worn piece of cardboard
up and over his shoulder
with skill and practiced nonchalance,
spinning it around his back
so fast I can't make out
the words written on it
without making eye contact.
Eventually he pauses
long enough for me to read,
A little kindness goes a long way.

Whenever I stop there I think of you,
wondering how you lived those last three years
asking myself
Were people kind to you?
Could they meet your gaze?
Where did you go when it rained?
Did you have a sign, too?
and if you did,
What did it say?

I NEVER STOPPED

I never stopped imagining he graduated college,
  his dream of film school, got a job at a big studio,
    worked his way into producing indie films,
     important documentaries.

I never stopped imagining him clean shaven,
  clear-eyed, arriving bashful at my front door bearing flowers,
    to tell me of a completed stint in rehab,
     his year or two of sobriety.

I never stopped imagining a moment
  when he showed true humility,
    apology and sincerity in his tone,
     hubris replaced with responsibility.

I never stopped imagining him
  in a lofty, light-filled space,
    his own art on the walls,
     charcoals resting on an open sketchbook.

We'd share a cup of tea, walk the dog by the water,
  ask about each other's lives. I'd hear of morning runs,
    his new love, how he now sees his children,
     is making the necessary repairs.

I never stopped imagining an unimaginable joy
  in being with him again——never stopped imagining
    the relief of sharing a long-awaited hug
     of homecoming.

I never stopped praying it wouldn't feel like betrayal
    to want reunion with all my heart, never stopped
    wanting him to stay for dinner, or stopped
    praying we could map a path to surrender
    allowing us to stand face to face, sentries at ease,
    each of us healed, each of us whole,
    spirits shining through our shared brown eyes.

PART II
MUD SEASON

The code for healing
lies in the DNA of the wound
as the regreening of the forest
is ignited by the fire that burns it.

Within the presence of beauty, fully received,
myths of regret cannot abide.

NAVIGATION

My father was a sailor.
He taught me to love the sea,
yet he failed to teach me
how to navigate
through a storm
so disorienting
the gravitational pull
of the world alters
rendering stars useless,
setting instrument dials
spinning.

I wish I could fashion cloth,
warm and sheltering,
under which our souls could rest
inhaling the smell of sweet, damp grass,
listening to distant waves,
the hoot of barn owl, howl of coyote,
to be flooded with moonbeams
awaiting a redemptive dawn,
for I am lost, weary
from this spinning.

MAKING MUD

2021 turned me to dust -
2022 was worse -
my bones
dust
my heart
dust
my understanding of the past
crushed
dust.
I wanted the wind to take it,
to take it all,
to take me.

When it rained
it flew down hard
across my windows,
ran under the house
down my face,
tears never
given time to dry
into tracks
on my cheeks.

Then mud,
thick, foul smelling, slippery,

I could not anticipate a lotus.
Footing treacherous
signage absent
stars obscured,
navigation by heartbeat.

What lies beneath
even further down
feels
numb, frozen
even on a balmy afternoon.

Lava finds the sea, volcanoes fill with water.
This will take time.

PRAYER OF DESCENT

From the beginning
your journey was one of descent
So I, too, will go down with you now,
    down
       down
         down
           down in
           to the cavern of my soul
           to the deepest part
           where it touches damp earth
           where I consigned you long ago
           when hope was truly lost.
Here in this blackness
I will lay flowers
  So, so many flowers
           blossoms of mercy, of redemption,
           each a prayer surrendered
           in shrouds of compassion,
           tear stained and woven by generations,
         each petal offered with a longing
         for the anguish and shame
         hidden in the crevices and seams
         where we have been grafted together
to be tended by hands larger than my own

to mulch and reseed
to grow and bloom
and to rise
on forgotten wings

to finally,
  finally
   fly
    free.

DEAR DEATH,

I know you must be busy with
with wars, diminishing habitats,
aging populations and such, but if you could spare
a moment, I have some questions.

Can I choose when you come? even just a little? or how?
Will I miss Earth?
Will I feel like I'm still here, even just a little?
Will I see my old dogs? find the cat that never came home
when my daughter was in 3rd grade?

Will there be incense smoke, or prayers by a river?
Will I hear my daughter crying as I pass?
Will my grandfather be there?
my grandmother?
my father?
my mother?
my birth mother?
Will we be able to communicate?
Will I understand them more fully when I see them?
Will I understand purpose and why
I was even in this life?

Will I see my son, Billy, again?
Will he be able to answer the heavy, looming questions?
Will those even matter?

Will my daughter be able to hear me, feel me watching over her,
feel my love for her from the other side of this veil?
Will the veil feel thinner, more translucent? Will I?
Will I understand silence?
Will I be able to hear the prayers of others?
Will my vigilance appear unneeded?
Do all these questions seem amusing?
Will I understand the joke?
How do you time your arrival, exactly?
How can you be so sure?
Are you more Kali or more Kwan Yin?
Will it feel like coming home?

Will I miss my body?
Will I have regrets? Was any of this real? or really necessary?
Will I have another chance to live? to do it better?
to make things right?
Did I make a difference?

Will I be able to welcome you with grace?

Wait, what was the point again?

Can I be a flower next time?

Is it all as simple as breath?

Will I finally get to fly?

MULCHING

I'm sorry for the half-eaten apple
not tossed to the bunnies
for the spinach, wilted, soupy and brown
found at the back of the produce drawer,
for the overripe avocado blackened
at the bottom of the checked bowl on the counter,
for the stone fruit pits
the orange peels
the moldy block of cheddar
thrown in the garbage. I'm sorry
for the half pot of Ethiopian coffee
poured down the drain
with the spoiled oat milk,
for the tops of leeks and carrots
that never made it to a stock pot,
and for using just a snip
of tender, precious basil,
only tiny sprigs of tarragon,
oregano, dill and mint,
those few slender chives,
chucking the rest.

I was distracted
by beauty, by bounty.
I wasn't thinking
of spoilage

Yet you, dear Mother,
received it all
mulching away, metabolizing
the overbought, the overlooked,
the terrible, smelly waste.
I'm sorry.
I had the best intentions.

Isn't the silent work of a mother
precisely this
continuous mulching
of more than outgrown clothes,
the spoiled fruit of unfavored toys,
again and again
tending and turning over life's debris,
seeding bruised hopes
into next season's fuel
again and again,

forever accepting
whatever comes
again and again
and again
and again
and again?

THE ARRIVAL OF DEATH

Death may come in an instant,
the hawk flying 200 miles per hour
grabbing you with its talons
to whisk you away
from everything you used to know
by heart,
arriving in a flash
like bad news
or a blinding awareness.

Death might slide in by imperceptible degrees
slithering in slow motion over years
that lose their numbers,
over minutes with far too many seconds
crammed into them,
blurring time
blurring memory
and blurring vision you just can't seem
to blink back
into clarity.

Death's most recent arrival
came waving its engraved invitation.
Darkness was its 'plus one'
who was not to be denied,
and the billion ton boulders
of grief that rolled through the door
bore no return address.

We forget
we are always dancing
under the disco ball of impermanence,
that everything reflected in its tiny, square mirrors
will turn to dust.

The task remains
accepting
what death undeniably delivered,
meeting its undiluted presence
with mine.

THE ARRIVAL OF LIFE

Life may come at you in a flash,
compressing time to an instant,
a hawk flying 200 miles per hour,
spiriting you away,
like good news or
some blinding awareness
changing how you see the world
and you don't know
where to look first
or what to do next.

Life might slide along
by imperceptible degrees, sinuous,
a languid crawl, stretching time
that unfurls in slow motion millimeters
over years that lose their numbers,
over days without names, time bending
around minutes containing miles,
creating memories soaked in details
you never want to fade away.

Life's most recent arrival
came waving its engraved invitation.
Brightness was its 'plus one'
who was not to be denied,
and the billions of baskets
of joy spilling their contents

through the door
bore no return address.
It was all mine
to claim.

We forget
we are always dancing
under the disco ball of impermanence,
that everything reflected in its tiny, square mirrors
will turn to dust.

The task remains
accepting
what life undeniably delivers,
meeting its undiluted presence
with mine.

AFTER THE FIRE

Forest skeleton
beauty's latest avatar
born of winter fire

A forest blackened
without needles, leaves or green
red glow at sunset

Forest skeleton
must I learn to love this too
black earth charred ground source

Forest skeleton
seeds burst forth from hidden stores
dark birth beneath burned land

Forest skeleton
newest shape of Mother's arms
poised to hold new life

UNKNOWING

I am birthing
comfort with not knowing
how to unravel
what has come before
where anything began
or why or how or with whom
or where to lay blame.
The deeper I look the more I see
those concepts cannot exist.
Each human expression
however brief
is glorious in its time.
Wind is leaf is tree is ground is root
and snake and music and bone,
and each will be the other
in its time.

Change and motion are primary, cyclical
essential composition embodied,
as elemental as fire, water,
air and earth,
absent polarities or projection
without beginning, without end or separation.
Relief will arrive, neither in silence
nor as a singular event;
rather it comes in waves, rolling

in rhythmic repetition reverberating
in our depths, perpetually meeting
revealing, mirroring our nature.

There is a sweetness,
an almost tangible freedom
in this budding awareness,
bringing with it
permission to be
wing
unfolded
rising.

THE UNKNOWN SPEAKS

Ahh, you're back again I see.
You seem to want something from me.
Questions in hand, your furrowed brow,
I cannot answer why or how.

I'd like to help, but I just can't,
no matter your debate, your rant.
Regardless how long life may be,
the telling is not up to me.
Conception's spark is mine to guard,
though I'll give Her your most kind regard.
Were my private, unheard stories told,
Your brain would certainly explode.

This *Being* is a masterstroke.
I swear it's not some cosmic joke.
This universe is ours to share,
but its secrets mustn't be laid bare.
Where'd the fun be if you knew
how it began, why it's askew,
why your world has come unglued
or why there's a pouch in the kangaroo?
You may forever ruminate,
but I shall not elucidate.
Is-ness is, and suchness such
Don't complicate it overmuch.
The answer will remain the same.
It's embedded in my name.

The vastness of my reach is great,
yet clues exist to excavate.
Perhaps somse hints can sweep your view,
shed light on parts of me in you.
You understand more than you know.
Be slow, in silence, let this grow.
Welcome stillness, meditate
and wisdom shall accumulate.
Trust your gut, your intuition.
There's no need for ammunition.
Balance doing with your being,
Make all your life an offering.

Make music, breathe, commune with trees.
Let beauty bring you to your knees
I've laid its glory at your feet
In ways audacious and discreet.
Lay your belly on the ground,
for Earth's advice is ever sound.
Feel sweet compassion's prize,
or fall into a lover's eyes.
Paint or weave or write or bake,
Remember there is no mistake.
When punches come, you've got to roll,
think more release, and less control.
Take yourself out on a date.
Play, imagine, just create.

Try sharing vulnerabilities,
Dream into possibilities.
Risk may foster innovation.
Awe insists on cultivation.
Go where you feel the most alive,
and do not fear the deeper dive.
Match nature's pace, consult your heart,
for there's no better place to start..
Offer thanks, lean into grace
for those are gifts we can't replace.
In doing so we'll most relate.
I grow through you. It is innate.

By now you've guessed there is no end,
so take a break, relax my friend.
I confound most understanding,
I'll forever keep expanding.
Settle in and be at ease,
watch a sunrise, feel the breeze.
Be at peace within my arms,
succumb to my delightful charms.
Precious One, just rest in me.
Enjoy our entangled destiny.
For I am you and you are me.
Surrender to the mystery.

P.S. Since we've concluded all our games,
please be so kind as to explain
why you've given me so many names?

DEAR POETRY,

Please change me
into the one who knows
she is the thrum under the silence,
who recognizes herself
as the space between the ticks
of her father's wind-up clock,
who knows herself as the pause
after an exhaled breath.

Change me
into the melting compassion
behind the wet gaze of the dog.

Dissolve my vigilance into softer noticing,
a deeper witnessing. Please
show me the pointed wingtip of crow at twilight,
show me its pristine and raucous iridescence
bowing and dipping at the outermost reach
of the cypress branch.

Poetry, please illuminate my way
in the darkest parts of the forest,
be the hand I hold as I learn its dense blackness.
Lead me along the path you know
lies hidden amid the debris.
Remind me. Fallen leaves and needles,
shed bark, broken branches and seed pods,
that moss and fern crushed under foot

fuel growth. Remind me, one more time,
of beauty's persistent renewal.
Hollow me out
so the bell at the heart of my being
rings clear. Please
keep whispering in my ear.

Help me uncover the essence of pearls
living within the grit of my fear.
Oh Poetry, make me more like you,
spontaneous, unexpected
grace scrawled on a napkin.
Please. I surrender. Name your price.
I no longer fear the cost of change.

RAIN TO ROOT

Mystery to spark
spark to love
love to womb
from womb to world
from formless to form,
this boy
to man
and father
and husband,
from husband to homeless
from man to body
from body to fire
from form to formless,
this man, my boy.

Body to ash
ash to sea
water to mist
mist to cheek
hand to cheek
you are still with me.

Mist to fog
to meadow
to trees
to hills
to my gaze
you are everywhere.

Mist to rain
rain to root
root to bud
bud to bloom
formless to form
once more
given by grace
governed by mystery.

EVENTUALLY

Eventually there is no more to say.

A heart slows,
Lungs take in less and less air.
Blips on a monitor stretch
further and further apart.
A doctor places a stethoscope on a chest
marking time of death
as the line on the screen flattens.

Eventually you release
the hand you were holding.

Eventually you won't wake up crying.

Eventually you won't resent the sun's rising.

Eventually the truth of death
won't be your first, jarring thought.

In time you put on clothes
with buttons
and zippers.
Eventually when someone asks,
"How are you?"
you won't dread answering,
and they won't worry
they said the wrong thing
when you do.

Eventually you won't avoid pictures
and you'll place them front and center
with flowers and a candle.

Food begins to smell good again
and you notice colors
other than grey, eventually.

A vast stillness
replaces the looping
questions in your head.

Eventually you meet someone
who walks with the same story.
Rage, grief and guilt
soften, eventually
resignation inches into acceptance.

Happy memories come.
You say yes to lunch,
a walk, or dinner and a movie.
You will again tolerate the laughter of others,
and eventually you're the one to crack a joke.
You might even
find yourself
singing in the car
instead of screaming.

Eventually the stone you swallowed
begins, grain by grain,
to dissolve.

Numbness fades.

Eventually your being adjusts
to its new configuration.

Anguish eventually relaxes
the vice grip it held
on everything,
and significance
rises like cream
over the top of randomness
and futility.

And eventually you may
find yourself
turning
toward a winter sun,
pausing to listen
to the church bells pealing
from across the meadow,
wrapping you
and your still beating heart
in the sweet,
green
promise
of possibility.

INCENSE

Offer incense to your grief.
Light it with the fire of your compassion
for yourself and for all that you grieve.
Its scent will permeate everything,
the way grief seeps into every cell.
As it burns, it transforms,
softening into fertile ash
to nourish your inner garden,
to sprinkle on the brokenhearted,
and as it burns, it turns into smoke
lifting your prayers skyward,
giving them wings.
So yes, offer incense to your grief.
Set it on fire.
Light it with the embers of your essence,
watch the glowing tip of this precious gift
reshape itself as it reshapes you,
and feel it alchemize
into love, into gratitude,
into praise for your life.

PART III
ROOTED & RISING

Rainbows touch down across the world.
There are so very many places
to find gold.

Windows
miles from the sun
glow pink with its rising.

NESTING

There is a dove
making its nest in the Japanese maple
outside my kitchen.

I want, with all my heart,
for it to be a positive omen,
a harbinger of peace
making its home here
within reach.

Perhaps grace is coming
to the stunned memories
yearning for ease.

Is this roosting
a precious gift of aliveness,
of self-compassion, delivered

by feathered messenger
twig by slender twig?

IN LIFE'S DANCE

Mystery leads.
We've been partners
for as long as I can remember,
perhaps even before that,
yet never seem to tire of one another.

When I flinch at its invitation,
or I resist its gentle pressure
at my back guiding me
where I prefer not to go,
I soften into a breath
that reminds me another will follow
and I bow,
eyes wide with amazement,
gather another fistful of petals
to offer to its untethered heart,
and I step
forward
to join the dance
with all that is
unknowable
wholly
holy.

SILENT WELCOME

How quiet it is!
Following a storm that left most of us
utterly powerless
I hear only the sound of the clock,
the dog's breath
and mine.
No cars on the road. No music playing. No voices raised.
The moon absent or hiding, the ocean impossibly inaudible.
All is dark, and ohh so very, very still.

I am aware of and breathing as the very essence
of this quiet, velvet blackness,
awake amidst a living dream, a meditative bliss.
It is as though I've reached some elusive, long sought after goal
without striving,
I've entered the essence of what lives here, inside of me, around me
holding me, breathing me,
where it and I have always been.
A remembered sense of arrival
meets me
extending itself to me and emerging, somehow, from me
in a welcome that includes every particle of my being.
Its embrace confirms what I had often hoped but never truly
believed –
unequivocal
irrevocable
belonging.

WATERFALLS

Imagine waterfalls
behind your eyes,
the meditation teacher suggests,
water cascading
down your body softening
your gaze relaxing
body and mind together.
All you need to do is breathe
and sit.

Sadness rebels, the mind
imagining the mud those waterfalls
will make, runoff from the last few years.

Yet a lotus is
because of mud
making flowers and leaves unseen
in the muck below the water's surface
for days, until one eventually breaks
the surface blooming
for simple joy,
each night returning
to its birthplace in the mud
rising again in the morning.
The seeds made in its core will be scattered
taking root nearby or elsewhere.
The flower cannot know how far
its life will reach.

I imagine
sitting
breathing
as lotus
seed
stem
as leaf
petal
root
and mud
expressing essence
never knowing its reach.

WEDNESDAY, 1 year, 10 months and 24 days after Tuesday

after "Sunday" by January Gill O'Neil

Wednesday—

You are the peak to ascend
  before the ease of a distant descent.
There are no odes written to honor you,
  no songs to sing your praises,
  no virtues to extoll.
Your moniker suggests
you have clearly dismissed
the principles of Phonics.

You are a hunker down day,
  your weight tethered to the workday.
  You are a do laundry and pay the bills sort of day,
  a day to sweep the front steps,
    to fold the sweater draped over the back of the chair,
    weed the yard and pick up the pup's medicine
from the vet. You are a check things
off the list type of day. Your melody is
  keystrokes and mouse clicks,
  car horns and ringtones, Wednesday.
There's not an ounce of vacation in you.

And yet, and yet Wednesday,
just last week you were
a wedding day, a new task for you,
decked out in your finery instead
of that camel's costume you're known to favor.
But there you were, love shining
in all her glory, beaming through every pore,
streaming long beams of happiness
through the redwoods.
I didn't know you had it in you.
Maybe you're a rebel in disguise.
Maybe we can relate.
Perhaps you offer a veiled invitation
to play.

So who knows?
Maybe anything is possible.

You sit betwixt and between, Wednesday.
You are just-before-the-after
and just-after-the-before. You are
the restless place, the always itching
mosquito bite of the unknown,
something requiring blood
and endurance.

What on Earth are we to do with you?

You are the door closed
on what's done,
on the life my son lived,
on the hope I still held for him,
on the forgiveness never given.
You are its hinge creaking
open, offering a glimpse of what may come,
an unplanned sweetness, an unknown gift
on the other side
of grief.

Perhaps you are an invitation
to let go.

Perhaps anything
is possible.

NACRE

Decades ago
my father cracked
open the shell of my childhood
stealing its pearl.

Decades later
my hands are filled
with pearls
made from the grit
he left behind.

I WILL NEVER BE

after Cristin DeVine

I will never be perfect.
I will never be thin enough, educated enough
or secure enough,
but that's not why I'm here.

I am here to re-inhabit, to reclaim and re-imagine.

I'm here to stand in awe and gawk at the immeasurable
beauty in this world,
and to reflect all of it back to you,
to your own heart through your own eyes.

I will never have a perfect home, the ideal sanctuary,
but I've learned that true safety is found in relationships
and has little to do with the objects around us.
My drinking glasses are probably spotted, whorls
of pet hair litter the floor, my morning teacup
and yogurt bowl sit unwashed in the kitchen sink,
but I have made peace with my ancestors,
and I use their legacy for good.

I may have too much jewelry, and shiny things
will always turn my head, but I've learned
that those won't buy happiness
and I won't be taking any of it with me.

The armor it has offered is thin compared
with the security that comes
from feeling part of the waves and sand, of salt air, being kin
to leaves whispering in the wind, or feeling my roots connected
to oak, in communion with crow and hawk and owl.

My dogs are thoroughly spoiled and bark at anything that moves,
but they show me how to be in the moment, teach me the
necessity of play and how to luxuriate in my body, inhabiting it
despite its sagging skin.
My hands are knobby from arthritis, wrinkled from the sun and
dry from the salt water I swim in, but they can work a camera,
show you the beauty of people and sacred traditions across this
globe, or they can cut up photos to make the struggle
and the stunning magnificence of the journey visible.
My hands can turn flowers into a Buddha.
Those same hands can walk with you
along the darkest path of grief.
They might be stiff and less nimble than they once were, but they
are here to envelope you in a genuine hug, arrange a bouquet
of roses, or cook you dinner or a fabulous dessert.
My hands are here to make offerings and build shrines.

I used to feel a caul of shame around me; thick, dark and cold,
but now I know I am made of mud and moon, mist and moss,
rust and rain, diamond dust and rolling hills.
My body is here for its own joy, to be nurtured and cherished,
passionately and reverently. It is safe in my hands.
My voice was silenced for many years, but I am here to reclaim it,
to teach, to counsel and to share.

I am here to speak the language of the soul, raw and true.
I am part grit and all heart.

I may not yet know all of why I am here, now,
 but I have grown more comfortable living with the mystery.
I'm here to accept life as it happens on its own terms.
I'm here to accept myself fully and unreservedly.
I'm here to reflect the sacred through my heart
and through my art.
I'm here to love, admire, and to gaze with wonder
at it all, with all of who I am.
I am here to heal, generations behind me,
not to simply exist or persevere or maintain a status quo
set by someone else.
I'm here to make wings that fly up from the ashes
of despair, to discover all of the places in myself
that have felt unworthy of affection
and love them unabashedly,
inviting you to do the same.
I'm here to receive the gift of breath.
I'm here to feel the grace of ground beneath my feet.
I am here to say thank you.

I WOULD BE

I would be grass
    meadow murmuring
for running and rolling
      and long, deep inhales
I would be water
    unfathomable
      in the simplicity of
        my two element composition
I would be laughter
    rich, full, deep,
from the belly
      releasing lightness
I would be prayer
    poem of longing and praise
      taken by breath
        straight to god.

IT COULD BE

It could be that you awaken on your first day of 2nd grade,
    or that today you are going to your college graduation,
    your wedding, your first job, to sign your first mortgage
    or to pick up your new dog from the shelter.
It could be that you're meeting a friend
    for tea or a walk, or heading out
    to milk the cow or to feed the chickens and gather eggs.

It could be that you awaken
    to the cry of your newborn child,
    to the final breath of your father,
    to the voice of your doctor calling
    with a diagnosis or a clear test result.

It could be that you're headed to the Ganges
    to bathe and make morning offerings under
    the ashy haze of the dead, burning just upriver.
It could be that you're on your way
    to the temple to spin prayer wheels or to the chapel
    to pray, counting your prayers on a string of beads,
    or about to fall into a line of monks
    to fill your begging bowl for the daily meal.
    You could be going to the lake
    to fill your net, or to the well to fill your bucket,
    to the field to fill baskets with the harvest. You could be
    waking under a mountain, in the forest, in the desert
    or at the sea,in a howling storm or under
    a clear, cerulean sky.

Wherever you are
between the poles of this planet
this day opens itself to you,
as any other in the daisy chain
of your becoming. Witnessing
its unfolding is grace,
surely — as surely as the miracle
of the first dawn
of the first day
under the first sky
perpetually rising within you.

PAUSE

under the heady influence of "Break" by Brooke McNamara

Rest here, dear one
Breathe
The worst of the work is done
for now
The dream dreaming you
has awakened you
in a new land
Relax
Though the rank breath of death
caressed your neck, raising gooseflesh
and ire, whispering for you to stay small,
to take comfort on the shore of the deadening familiar,
you dove in.
Trust
The song singing you
added a verse, tweaked the chorus and changed keys,
and while the tune feels awkward in the mouth,
it asks of you what it has always asked -
be present, sing into both the ache
and the beauty.
The coda is still being written.
Breathe
The dance dancing you
still woos you, though its steps, too, are new.

Remember
you have learned to trust the tango
of darkness, to trust the salt tide
of your tears has dissolved into the blood
of your becoming. You learned to trust gravity
vibrating with aliveness in your bones
continually drawing you down, wrapping you
into the rich embrace
of this Earth.
Rest
You are held.
You are never alone.

LEAN IN

Make your life
      an offering to the
      poetic to the
      unknowable to the
      unnamable to
   beauty, unending,
   to challenge lean in
      to grace

Bring your hands
      to your heart
exhale
      bow your head
be
      the essential
      prayer
      of your life.

URGENCY

It happens in the span of a week,
the dormant rises,
entire hillsides full of spring.
Do you ever feel it,
an urgency to bloom,
to bend your being
toward light?

OHH! THE BELLS

that rang that morning, those monastery bells
that rang and kept on ringing,
speaking to me of life,
their tolling entering me, reverberations
resonating deep in my bones, recalibrating
the whole of me to the planet's pulse,
utterly disarming complacency, finding the melting point
of shame and dissolving separateness, a shamanic smudge
of tone and vibration working its way into the defended
muscle behind my ribs, shaking loose
what had hardened there, answering
an unspoken prayer, leaving only breath
and presence. The longer they rang
the more I was hollowed, my body ringing.

I listen for them now, mornings
and afternoons. Each time I hear them clang
is another chance to open, to dare feeling
as fully as I did that morning, each time
an invitation to welcome
the potency of aliveness,
the heady rush of joy.

For Barbara Ranier

WONDER AND WOUNDING

What is loved
searingly beautiful
unthinkable
too painful to bear
will all break

you, break us
open
life's chisel cracking
the rock of us
revealing gems
where emptiness has been.
Grit flows
insistent,
pressure and time
polishing spirit,
our own light
beaming through
every crystalline point,
reshaping us,
making us ever more radiant
by both
the wonder and the wounding.

LAKE OF TEARS

I've never much liked the Pride of Madeira
plants growing in profusion here
on the coast, especially the blue ones.
My new house has them in droves. I prune,
I snip and trim and dig, yet each year
they return, thick and proud.

This spring on the warm day before our last
good rain, I notice the monarch approaching, the bees
along with the hummingbirds, darting and dipping to drink
of the sweetness tucked in to those closely clustered
blossoms. I set down my shears,
understanding the gift of those spikey blooms,

the way I came to understand, in the flash of a wing,
that the tears of grief I have cried
have all gathered,
forming a deep lake
where moonlight freely dances.

LIVING KINTSUGI

*Literally meaning "to join with gold," kintsugi is the
Japanese art of repairing broken pottery or glass with gold.*

Rounding the bend at the top of the hill
overlooking the last turn in the river
a field of melted stars unfolds, gold
flooding my vision between feet and sky,
mustard in full bloom.

Seeing with my eyes, I take its measure
with my heart, a broken cup
in the hands of a kintsugi master
repairing its cracks, filling
the fracture between breath and bone
with the lavish brilliance of the field.

Oh! it nearly hurts, this beauty,
rousing the exhausted organ
alive again. I stand ever more fully
for the breaking, open to all
the spring yet to come.

WHAT I SAY

after Deena Metzger

I say
I am an aging woman
young enough to believe
I can hold a lake full of moonlight
in my broken heart

I say I rest here
where silence lives
nestled into stillness and chaos alike

I say I live here
in a breath
in a body
where love and emptiness collide

I say I dance
in continual sway
in tandem
with all that lives,
where the whole of life is contained
in this blade of grass
this droplet of ocean spray
this pinprick of light

I say
within this silence
my heart unwinds
unfurling as coiled fern
into a morning sun

I say in this moment
I am alive, dying
into what made me
with each exhalation

I say in this moment
there is nothing
and everything that was
and is and will be
all at once.

ENVELOPED

Fog walked across the street at mid-day,
graceful as a whisper
like my 92-year-old neighbor in her blue parka,
head bowed to the wind, determined
to cover miles of ground.

Under the rolling blanket, earth and sky merged
in the wild embrace of lovers too long apart, eager
to reclaim every inch of the other.
The landscape, fully enfolded, altered.
Everything everywhere, fog.

I want to remember
how it felt to be
utterly enveloped,
how it felt to be both
lover and beloved,

remember
how it was
to feel my way home.

For Barbara Ranier

VOICES OF GOD

shaman's whistle

snowflakes swirling

wind blowing

leaves rustling

monks chanting

lone flute singing

choir soaring

dog dreaming

wings fluttering

heart beating

lungs breathing

ecstasy peaking

rain falling

waves thundering

grievers wailing

hawk calling

children laughing

petals dropping

silence

ENDNOTES

IMAGINE!: Quoted from Dr. Maya Angelou's appearance on OWN Network's show "Oprah's Master Class" in 2011. The phrase originally comes from the 1931 song *"God Put a Rainbow in the Clouds"* written by Andrew Jenkins.

IN THE LONG DARK: *The Long Dark* is a phrase from author, therapist and soul activist Francis Weller, found in his foreword to Duane Elgin's book *Choosing Earth, At the Threshold: Grief, Initiation, and Transformation,* ©2022 Duane Elgin.

The words "some fire, some honey" were inspired by a Sojourner review of Denise Levertov's book *This Great Unknowing, Last Poems,* a collection of her final poems, describing her words as 'honey and fire on the tongue'.

YOU LIVE IN ME: After "I Wear You" ©2023 by Susan Vespoli appearing in her book *One of Them Was Mine,* Kelsay Books, American Fork, UT

TUESDAY: After "Sunday" in *Rewilding,* ©2018 by January Gill O'Neil, CavanKerry Press Ltd., Fort Lee, New Jersey.

I NEVER STOPPED: with a nod to "My Son No Longer Missing" ©2022 by Susan Vespoli, appearing in *Blame It on the Serpent,* Finishing Line Press, Georgetown, Kentucky.

PRAYER OF DESCENT: The words "forgotten wings" from Pablo Neruda's poem "Poetry" or "La Poesia" found on www.wordsfortheyear.com, August 6, 2017.

WEDNESDAY: After "Sunday" in *Rewilding*, ©2018 by January Gill O'Neil, CavanKerry Press Ltd., Fort Lee, New Jersey.

I'LL NEVER BE, written after *I'll Never be Perfect* by Cristin DeVine, unpublished.

IT COULD BE: the phrase *the first sky* is from the poem *"One Heart"* © 2001 by Li-Young Lee appearing in *Book of My Nights*, BOA Editions, Ltd.

PAUSE: written after "Break" ©2020 by Brooke McNamara appearing in *Bury the Seed, poems for releasing more life into you*, Performance Integral, Boulder, CO.

WHAT I SAY: Written after "I Wrote a Love Letter Without Words," © 1989 by Deena Metzger. The words "love and emptiness" are from her poem "That Philosophical Sadness that Comes Down in the Dawn. Both appear in her book *Looking for the Faces of God*, Parallax Press.

GRAMERCIES

from the French grand merci, big thanks

Immense grief pendulates with immense gratitude, and there are many to thank.

My precious daughter Stephanie, thank you. You have borne the ugliest parts of your lineage with strength and grace. You have been my best friend, spiritual companion, sister and teacher since day one. There is no one on this Earth I would rather sit with at a counter eating chowder, writing a poem about pie, or drive with, belting out an Annie Lennox tune under a full moon, than you.

Francis Weller, thank you for your kindness, for your fierce compassion and for the countless hours you have devoted to bringing your gifts to this needy world. As a teacher, community builder and soul activist, you are unsurpassed. I wouldn't have been able to turn toward grief without the foundation you provided. I will always hold you in the utmost esteem and with the deepest gratitude. To Judith Weller, you are irreplaceable, gifted, wise and loved.

To Amy Somers, Rob Somers and Robin DeFilippi, friends par excellence, thank you for holding my hands and my heart through the darkest times. You have checked on me during storms, taken me to the emergency room, sat through surgery. You know which drawer has the corkscrew, which cupboards hold the Tupperware and, have been inexhaustible supporters of my healing and creative journeys. Thank you for the laughter and the wisdom. Thank you for sharing your wide open hearts and your shiny spirits. Tim, welcome to the band. Hold on for a wild, joyful ride.

Thank you to Cristin DeVine and Peter Fonken for opening your home and your hearts on countless occasions, for sharing abundant talents and kindnesses with sincerity and generosity. Thank you for loving and tending the land. Thank you for Playlist 14. Thank you for encouraging my poetry and for reminding me that there is always more than my story. Dear Pedro, giving your time to the careful reading of this manuscript was indispensable and invaluable. Please know I am forever grateful. You are both shining examples of living in authenticity, embodying all the gifts of your bountiful, wild natures.

For her deep and careful listening with immense presence and tenderness, I offer immeasurable thanks to Brooke McNamara. Though we have yet to meet in person, I couldn't love or respect you more. I am in awe of your mothering, your talents, your devotion to your practice and to your family. You are a true gem. Your influence is felt throughout this book. Thank you for your time and encouragement and for sharing your brightness with us all. Three deep bows.

Sarah Saxby, you are a treasured and faithful friend. From parenting toddlers to being the mothers of adult children, from knees to ashes, you have been there. Thank you for endless kindness.

To Cat McDowell thank you for your quiet inspiration and for listening to my early efforts.

Thank you to Mercy Galarza for always being on the other end of the phone. Life wouldn't be the same without your stories and our conversations.

Thanks also to Lisa Tarsitano, my support in the gym for so many years. You tolerated my sense of humor, my petulant inner child. You were often the first to hear the worst of my news, and your heart was always open. What a gift!

Thank you to Ginna and David Gordon for their support and skill in getting this book to print. How lovely you both are and how beautiful your attention and your work.

All blessings and gratitude to Jennifer Allen and to Cindy Stein for working your magic.

Thank you to Sophie for teaching me to run straight into life and to Bodhi for his floof, his love of cheese, for all the walks, and for sleeping on my pillow. Bo, with a thousand nicknames, you are breathing, living love, a cherished companion.

Thank you to the Carmelite Monastery for the faithful touchstone of the bells.

To the ancestors, human and non-human, named and unknown, whose lives support mine, deep honor and endless thanks.

Lastly, and always first, I offer my deepest gratitude to the Great Mystery and to the land upon which I live: Ohlone, Costanoan, Rumsen and Esselen land that has nourished and dreamed me while utterly disarming me with its beauty. It has freely offered ceaseless wisdom, inspiration and sanctuary. It is home to the messengers, to the ancestors and to my heart, eternally.

ABOUT THE AUTHOR

Kim Birdsong is a collage artist, photographer, and counselor.

For 16 years she served survivors of sexual assault through her local rape crisis center. She maintains a limited private practice and conducts small and large group grief rituals and workshops.

She believes that a creative response to profound pain can foster healing for both an individual and for the community.

Kim lives in Carmel, California with her labradoodle, Bodhi.

This is her first volume of poetry.